Mediaeval and Modern Coins in the Athenian Agora

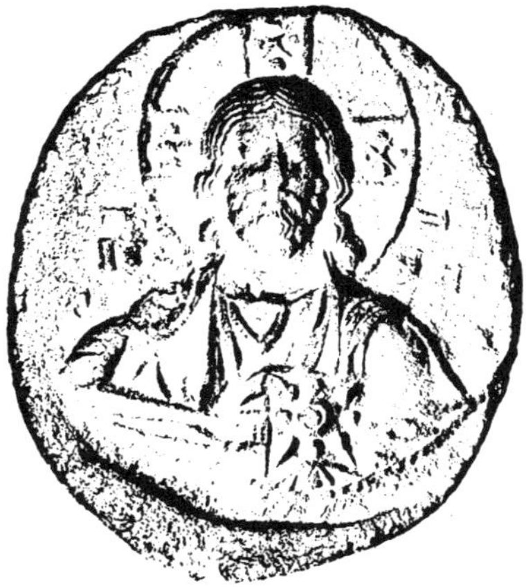

AMERICAN SCHOOL OF CLASSICAL STUDIES AT ATHENS

PRINCETON, NEW JERSEY

1978

THE ATHENIAN AGORA has been more or less continuously inhabited from prehistoric times until the present day. During the American excavations over 75,000 coins have been found, many dating as early as the 6th century B.C., when coins were first used in Athens. Much of this money is ancient and furnishes valuable evidence for reconstructing the life of the Greco-Roman city. The numismatic finds include, however, a considerable amount of material from the mediaeval and modern periods—coins of the Byzantine emperors, of the Frankish, Venetian, and Turkish conquerors, of modern Europe, and of Greece itself. These mediaeval and modern excavation coins provide a record of the kind of money used in the Athenian market place for some 1,650 years—from the early 4th century after Christ, when Christianity was adopted as the official religion of the Roman Empire, to today. The coins tell us a great deal about the commercial and political history of Athens throughout the centuries.

The coins uncovered by the American excavators do not, however, give us a complete picture of coinage in Athens, because nearly all of the coins found are bronze or copper pieces of small change. The silver and gold coins which circulated in the city are rarely encountered because the excavation coins represent almost exclusively coins which were lost and never recovered—stamped into the earth floor of the Agora, or dropped in wells, drains, or cisterns. When coins of precious metal were dropped they were searched for until found. There are, of course, exceptions to this rule, but most of the silver and gold coins illustrated in this book come from hoards—groups of coins intentionally secreted, usually during times of trouble, and never recovered by their owners. One such hoard (of copper coins) is illustrated (7) and others are mentioned throughout the text. Coin hoards are often of more value to the numismatist and historian than individual pieces, because they document the kinds of coins that circulated together in a specific place at a specific time.

THE MAKING OF COINAGE

ALL THE MEDIAEVAL and some of the modern coins illustrated in this book were handmade. The method of striking (used also in ancient times) was quite simple and required only a few basic tools (1). The first step was the preparation of the flan, or metal blank, upon which the coin designs would be stamped. Flans could be produced in a number of different ways, and the Agora finds document a few of these. Often the metal was heated to

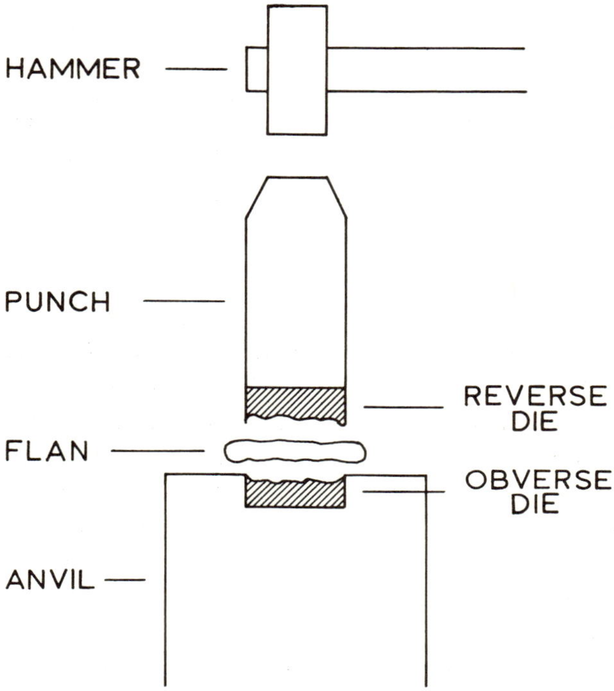

1. Method used for hammered coinage before the invention of modern minting machinery. Designs were cut into two dies and hammered into a flan to produce a coin.

a molten state and then poured into a series of connected disk-shaped molds. Some of the coins reproduced here show the casting 'lugs' that were never removed and attest to the use of this method. Casting, either in such circular molds or in globular form, was generally used for coins of precious metal. These pieces were accepted in commerce at their bullion value and casting produced flans of fairly uniform weight. Exact weights were later attained by testing each blank, filing the heavy ones, and remelting the light ones. Copper and bronze coins were, on the contrary, of token value only, and less precise means of preparing coin blanks could also be employed. One common method was to cast or forge by hammering metal rods and then cut individual flans from them, either by repeated chisel strokes or by sawing. Blanks so obtained might vary considerably in size and, although the mint authorities were undoubtedly instructed to produce a certain number of coins per pound of metal, in practice individual coins of base metal of the same date, denomination, and mint are only of approximately the same diameter, thickness, and weight. Western mediaeval coin blanks were normally obtained by cutting up hammered sheets of metal with shears.

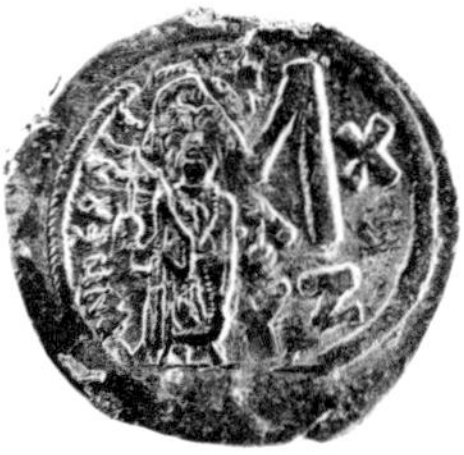

obverse

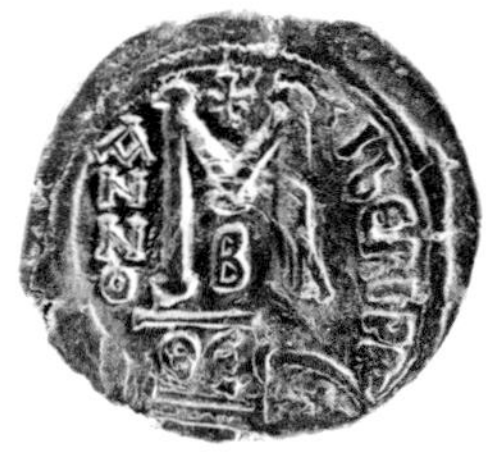

reverse

2. An 'overstruck' Byzantine coin. The piece was first issued under Maurice Tiberius (582–602) and later reissued with new types under Heraclius (610–641).

To stamp images on the prepared flans, it was necessary to cut dies—negative designs—usually in iron or a very hard bronze alloy. Coin dies were of two types. The lower die, which bore the image (usually of a ruler) of the obverse face of the coin, was fixed in an anvil or block of wood. The upper die, which produced the reverse type of the coin, was cut at the end of a punch. The craftsmen who engraved coin dies were sometimes first-rate artists. In modern times their designs are frequently signed and signatures even appear on some ancient coins. Dies were generally systematically destroyed by the mints because of their value as tools for coining money. There are, e.g., no surviving Byzantine dies despite nearly a millennium of coin striking, although some Western mediaeval dies have come down to us.

In the final stage of the minting process the prepared flan was placed on top of the obverse die and the punch die was centered above it. The workman then pounded the upper die with a hammer, thereby producing impressions on both sides of the coin simultaneously. Several blows were often necessary to obtain clear designs because in mediaeval times the blanks were usually struck while cold and hard, rather than heated and malleable as was generally the case in antiquity. Mediaeval records and recent experiments with modern dies suggest that the average handmade die could produce about 10,000 or more coins before breaking.

Sometimes the laborious process of preparing new flans for striking was avoided by the re-use of old coins. Often the old coin types were not entirely obliterated by the new types and such coins, with two or more successive images visible, are said to be 'overstruck'. A good example of an overstruck coin is illustrated here (2)—a Byzantine copper coin of the emperor Heraclius issued around A.D. 615 struck over a piece of Maurice Tiberius dated A.D. 591. The Heraclian types are, on the obverse, two standing figures (one is clearly visible) and, on the reverse, a large M (the denomination: 40 nummi) accompanied by other letters and numbers. The 'undertypes' (the designs of Maurice Tiberius) are a bust of the emperor (barely visible, although the name Tiberius is clearly legible at the right) and a similar M on the other side of the coin. (The new obverse type was thus struck over the old reverse type, and the new reverse type over the old obverse.) Such overstruck coins have been of great value to scholars in establishing the sequence of striking of series which are not otherwise datable, e.g., the so-called Anonymous Byzantine coinage discussed below (p. 15). The great number of overstruck 'anonymous' Byzantine coins found in the Agora excavations have, in fact, been of crucial importance in establishing the chronology of that series.

Another means of altering old coins for new purposes is called countermarking. Countermarking was a means of reissuing coins even more economical than overstriking because only a small design is stamped on the old coin, usually just on one side. Countermarks could be used for a variety of purposes—to render foreign coins legal tender for local transactions, to distinguish between genuine and counterfeit coins, to change the value of a coin, etc. A coin of the Byzantine emperor Constans II found in the Agora (3) was countermarked on the obverse with a small monogram under Constantine IV, probably to revalue the coin at half its former value. At the time the piece was countermarked new coins of the same denomination were being struck at about twice the weight of those issued under Constans II. In this case the countermarking process has almost obliterated the reverse type, but this is not an inevitable result.

The old method of producing coins by hammering was gradually supplanted in Europe from the 16th century on. Refinements in design over the centuries have resulted in machines capable of manufacturing thousands of coins per minute. In addition to increased speed of striking and the other obvious benefits derived from the replacement of human labor by machines, modern coining presses have three important advantages over the hammered method: the production of exactly circular blanks of uniform weight; the stamping of the blanks with clear, perfectly centered designs; and the marking of the edges of the coins with grooves or letters (or both) to insure against the reduction of a coin's metal content by filing. In the early 19th century machines were invented that permitted dies to be produced mechanically by reducing a metal cast of an artist's original large plaster model. Thus today an infinite number of identical dies, each capable of striking about 80,000 coins, can be made from a single model about ten inches in diameter.

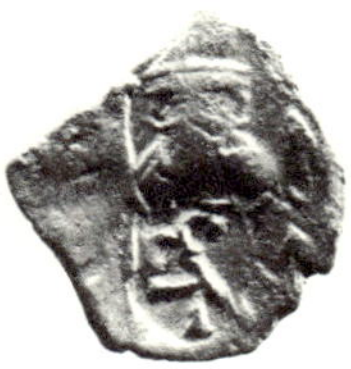

obverse

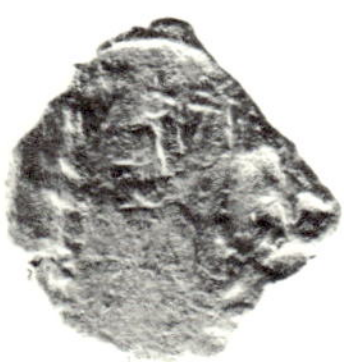

reverse

3. A 'countermarked' Byzantine coin. A small monogram was impressed upon a coin of Constans II (641–668) under Constantine IV (668–685) in order to devalue the coin.

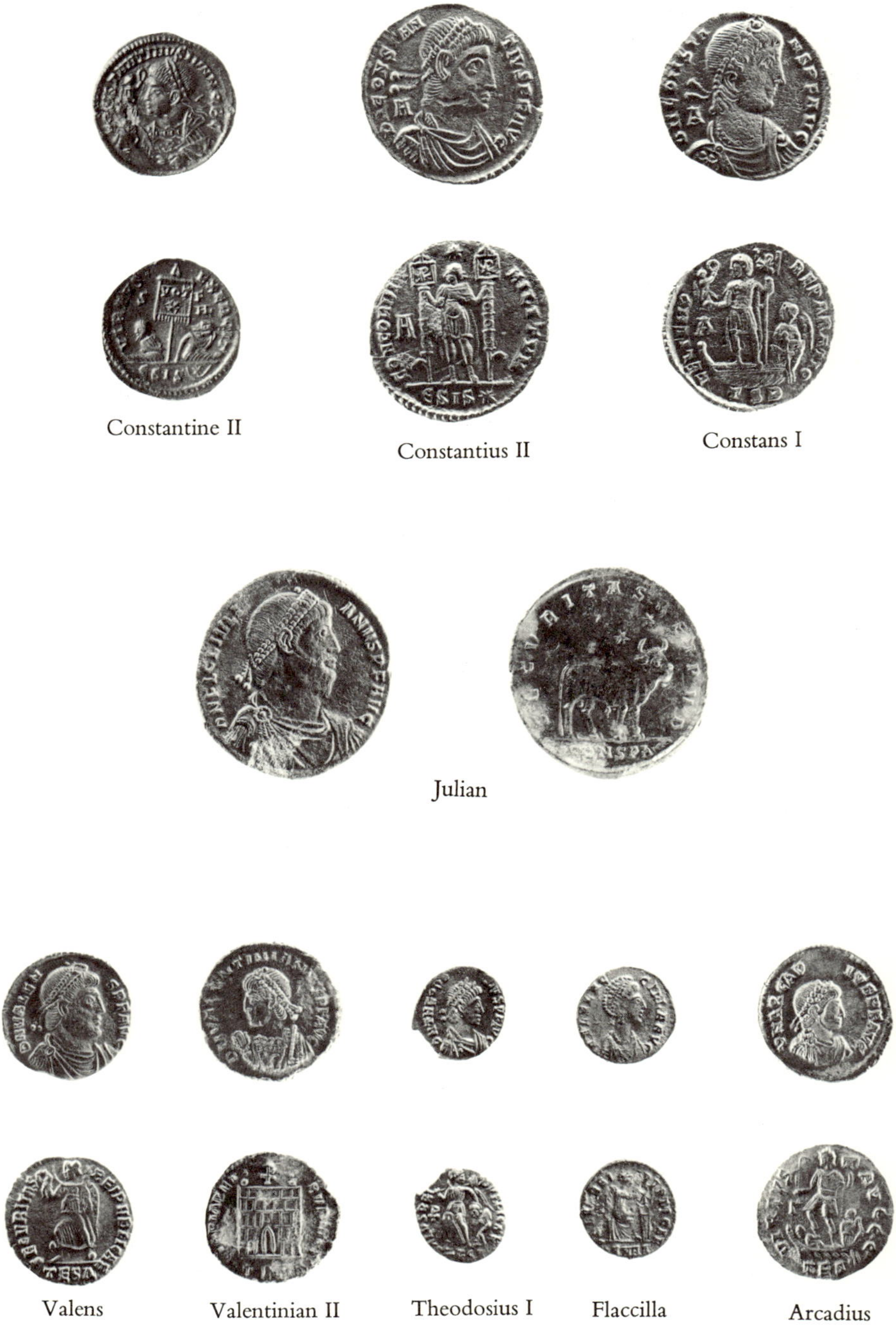

4. 4th-century Roman bronze coins.

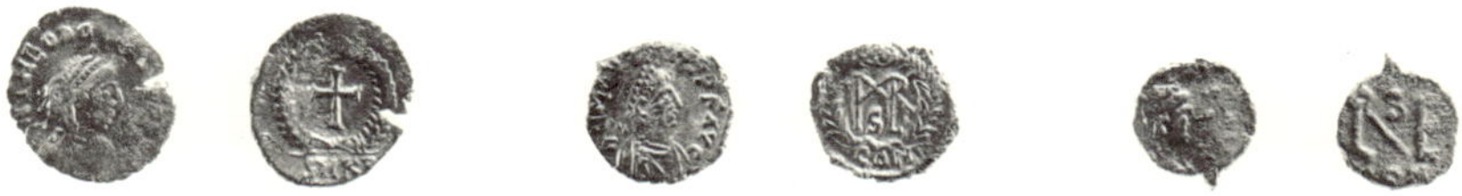

Theodosius II Marcian Leo

5. 5th-century Roman bronze coins.

LATE ROMAN COINAGE

OPINION is divided as to when the ancient world came to an end and the Middle Ages began, but a strong case can be made for 11 May 330, the day the Roman emperor Constantine dedicated the city of Constantinople to the God of the Christians. The transition from 'ancient' to 'mediaeval' was, of course, gradual. There is, in fact, no significant change in the Roman coinage after 330. Late Roman gold, silver, and bronze coins are, like those of the first three centuries after Christ, stamped with the bust and titles of the emperor or a member of his family on the obverses, and almost exclusively pagan types on the reverses.

In the Agora excavations late Roman gold and silver coins are unknown, but thousands of bronze pieces of small change have been unearthed. A dozen of the finest specimens are reproduced here (4, 5). They bear portraits of the three sons of Constantine, joint regents after 337, some of the major figures of the Valentinian and Theodosian dynasties of the late 4th century, and three of the emperors of the 5th century. The reverses are primarily military in character, portraying Victory personified, bound captives, the emperor with military standards, a fortified camp gate, etc. Overtly Christian types, such as the cross in wreath of Theodosius II, are rare, although allusions to the new state religion appear: Victory inscribes the chrismon (the monogram composed of the initial letters of Christ's name in Greek) on a shield on a coin of Flaccilla, and the monogram is placed on other reverses above the camp gate, on military standards, and next to Victory dragging a captive. An exceptional type is the sacred bull of Apis on the large bronze piece of Julian 'the Apostate' who attempted to revive pagan worship in the mid-4th century.

The bronze pieces of the 4th century were issued in four different denominations, but in the 5th century only the tiny bronzes called nummi were struck. Since silver coins were issued in very small quantities during this period, there were, in practice, no coins intermediate in value between the nummi and gold pieces worth literally thousands of times as much. This unfortunate situation was not remedied until the Anastasian currency reform of 498.

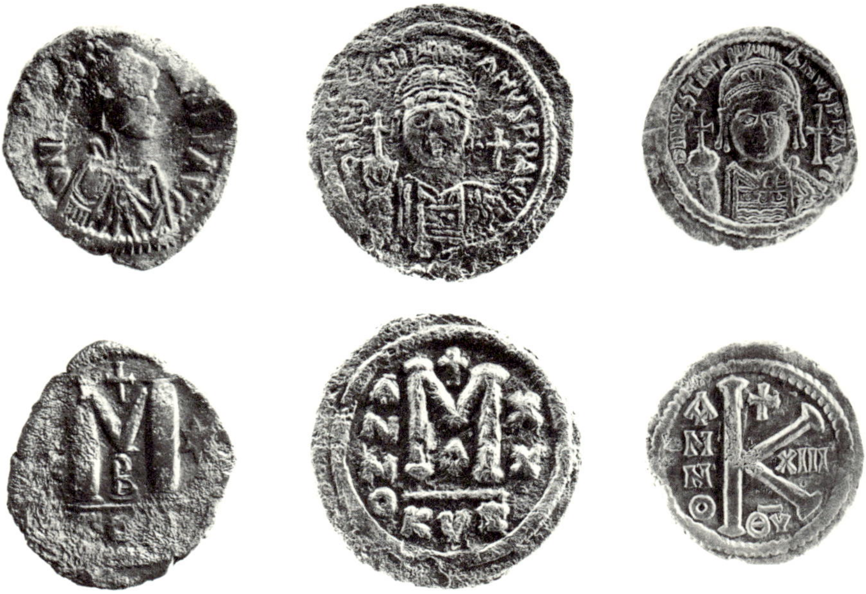

6. Copper coins of Anastasius and Justinian.

BYZANTINE COINAGE

THE BEGINNING of Byzantine coinage is universally reckoned from the outset of the reign of the emperor Anastasius (491–518), although his monetary reform was not instituted until 498. The Anastasian reform primarily affected the copper coinage and was designed to rectify the problems arising from the absence of pieces of small change higher in value than one nummus. Because the American excavations have brought to light thousands of Byzantine copper coins (but only one silver piece and no gold coins), the reform of 498 and all important subsequent changes in the Byzantine copper coinage can be illustrated by the Agora finds.

Under Anastasius copper multiples were reintroduced in the form of 40-, 20-, 10-, and 5-nummus pieces. The new copper coins (6) retained the traditional obverse profile bust of the emperor accompanied by the Latin legend 'Our Lord Anastasius forever emperor', a formula also used on Roman bronzes of the 4th and 5th centuries. The standard Greco-Roman practice of placing a pictorial type on the reverses was, however, abandoned in favor of a large numeral indicating the coin's denomination and a variety of small symbols and letters telling, among other things, the name of the city and section of the mint (officina) that struck the coin. The numerals used on the

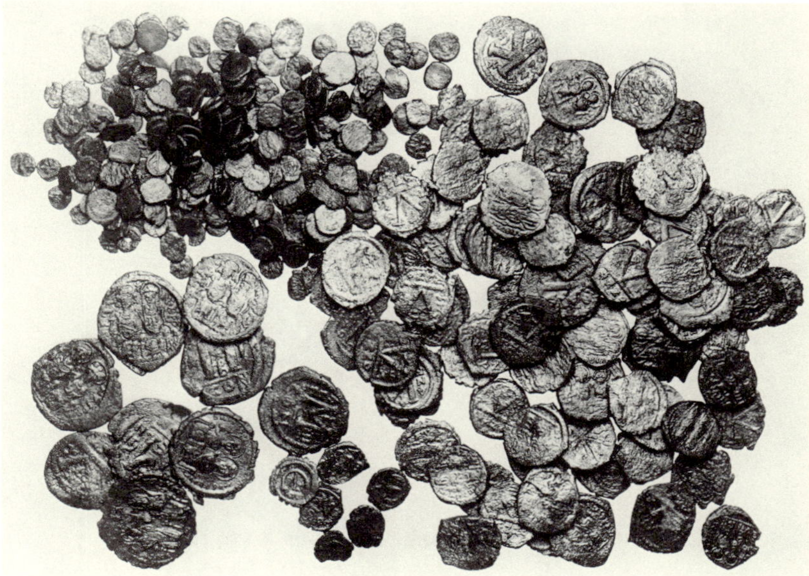

7. A hoard of Byzantine coins buried *ca.* A.D. 580.

early Byzantine coins are Greek, despite the obverse Latin legend and the use of Latin letters for the mint signature: M (40), K (20), I (10), Є (5). The new denominations were called the follis, half-follis, dekanummion, and pentanummion respectively.

The expanded range of denominations introduced under Anastasius may be illustrated effectively by a hoard of 341 copper coins found along the Panathenaic Way in 1971 (7). The hoard was buried around 580, almost a century after the Anastasian reform, and contains about 100 folles, half-folles, and pentanummia, and about 250 nummi. The Agora deposit is one of several hoards buried in Athens during the early 580's which attest to an attack on the city by Slavic invaders, causing the frightened populace to hide money from the looters.

Important modifications to the Anastasian system were made under Justinian (527–565). A larger, heavier follis was introduced (6) and a full-face bust replaced the profile portrait of the emperor on the obverses. The information given on the reverses was, after 538, expanded to include the date, as well as the mint name and officina number. The dates are given in regnal years and preceded by the Latin word *anno*. Illustrated are a follis (M) of Kyzikos (KYZ) struck in officina 1 (A) in the twentieth year (XX) of Justinian's reign, and a half-follis (K) of Antioch (ΘV̄) struck in year 13 (XIII). The monogram used as the Antioch mint signature is an abbreviation of

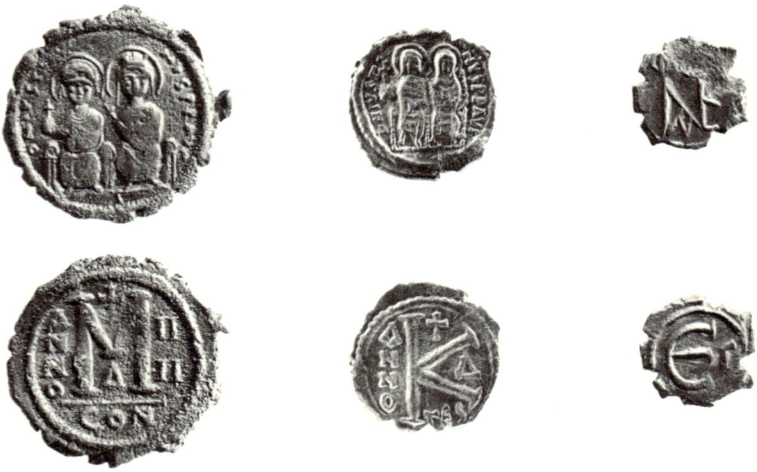

8. A follis, half-follis, and pentanummion of Justin II and Sophia.

Theoupolis (City of God), the name the Syrian city assumed after a great earthquake in 528. More mints were in operation under Justinian than at any other time in Byzantine history—a testimony to the extent of the emperor's military campaigns.

Justinian was childless and was succeeded by his nephew Justin II (565–578) who married Sophia, niece of Theodora, Justinian's wife. During Justin's reign the size and weight of the copper coins were reduced sharply (8). The obverses of the new folles and half-folles portray both the emperor and empress with nimbus and seated on a double throne. The smaller field available to the artist on Justin's pentanummia was not suitable for an elaborate double imperial portrait and legend, and so a monogram made up of the Greek letters of the words 'Justin and Sophia' replaced the pictorial type. The reverses of Justin's folles and half-folles continue to furnish the date, officina number, and mint (Constantinople and Thessalonica respectively for the illustrated pieces); the reverses of the pentanummia give only the officina number.

Further minor modifications of the Byzantine copper coinage took place during the late 6th and 7th century (9). On the reverses of the folles of Tiberius II (578–582) a cursive **m** replaces the angular version. The emperor is portrayed alone on the obverses of all his folles and half-folles, with the exception of the half-folles struck at Thessalonica, where he is shown enthroned next to the empress Anastasia. The copper coins of Phocas (602–610) are distinguished by the first attempt on Byzantine coins at true portraiture; the emperor is shown with a short, pointed beard. On the reverses the value of

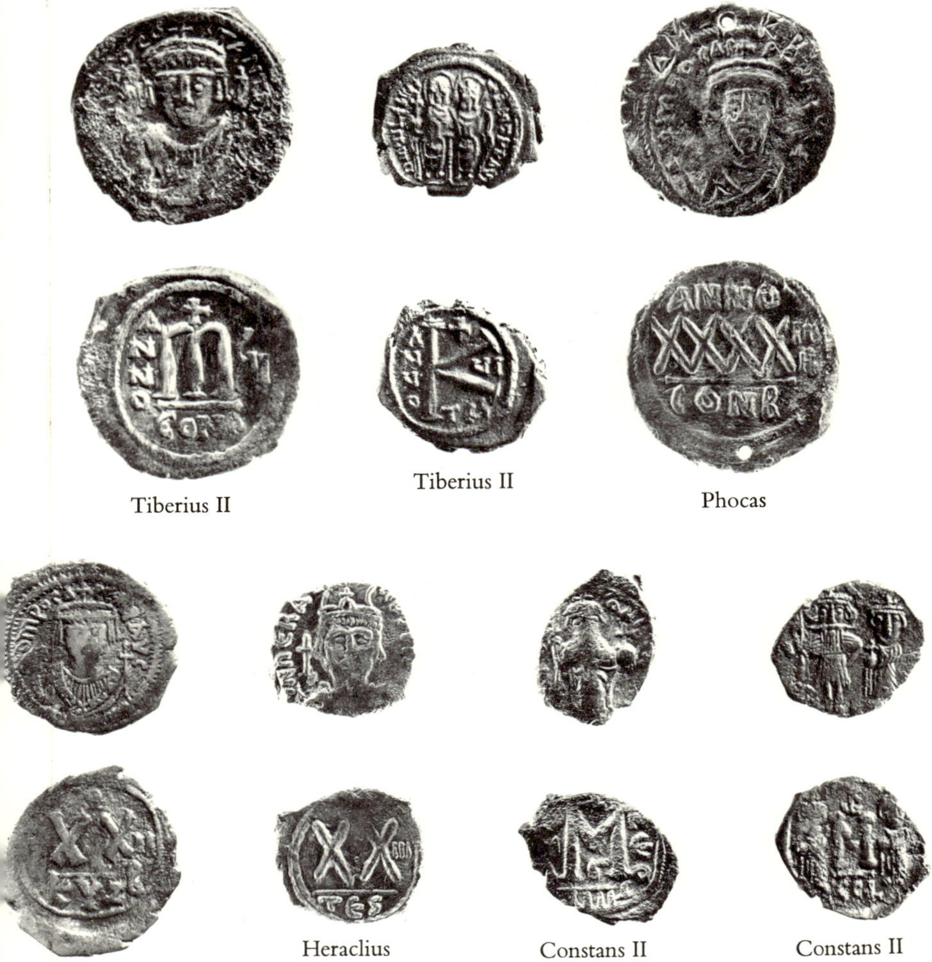

Tiberius II — Tiberius II — Phocas

Phocas — Heraclius — Constans II — Constans II

9. Late 6th- and 7th-century Byzantine copper coins.

the coin is now given in Roman rather than Greek numerals. The illustrated follis of Phocas was, at a later date, pierced and used as a pendant, and initials (of two lovers?) were scratched into the obverse above the imperial effigy. Greek numerals are again used to mark denominations on almost all the coins of Heraclius (610–641), but there are exceptions, like the illustrated half-follis from Thessalonica. The new interest in portraiture led to the issuance of coins which recorded changes in the emperor's appearance; Heraclius is depicted wearing both a short and a long beard. During the 7th century the weight-standard of the Byzantine coinage was progressively lightened, less care was taken in the striking of the coins, and inflation led to the almost total suspension of production of the lower denominations. The copper coinage of Constans II (641–668), who was crowned emperor shortly before his 11th birthday, is of poor quality and limited almost solely to folles of greatly reduced weight. They are remarkable for the introduction of two legends in Greek, meaning: 'by this sign [of the Cross] may you conquer' and 'renovation'. The obverse types vary considerably. Constans may appear alone, as on the illustrated follis from Constantinople, or with his three sons, as on the Agora piece struck at Syracuse, where the emperor spent the last five years of his life.

During the 8th century Athens seems to have been little more than a provincial village and few coins datable to this period have been discovered in the Agora. It is not until the 10th century that the city recovers economically and that coins reappear in quantity in the American excavations. Nevertheless, enough 9th-century pieces have been found to document a major change in the Byzantine copper coinage (10). Under Theophilus (829–842) the striking of denominations lower than the follis was all but discontinued and value marks were dropped from the coins. The new reverses were stamped with inscriptions, usually of four lines and containing both Greek and Latin letters and words. The epigraphic reverse designs had been introduced earlier on the Byzantine silver coinage and are ultimately based on Arab coins. The inscriptions are formulaic in character and no longer record the date of issue or the mint. The folles of Theophilus read 'Theophilus Augustus may you conquer' and those of his successors regularly proclaim the ruler 'by the grace of God, emperor of the Romans'.

The obverse types of the 9th- and 10th-century copper coins (10) continue to portray the reigning emperor, and sometimes his imperial colleagues as well. Basil I (867–886) appears both alone and with his son Constantine. Leo VI 'the Wise' (886–912) is also portrayed alone and with his younger brother Alexander. Romanus I (920–944), an admiral, came to power by force while Constantine VII, nephew of Alexander, was only a child, and had his image placed on the coinage. The illustrated follis on which Constantine VII (913–959) appears in his own right was struck after Romanus was exiled in 944.

The only Byzantine silver coin to come to light in the Agora (10) is a miliaresion of John I (969–976) on which the inscription proclaiming John as emperor of the Romans is placed on the obverse and the imperial portrait is relegated to the center of the reverse and circled by the formula 'Jesus Christ conquers'. The miliaresion had been introduced by Leo III in 720; in the 10th century its value was equal to that of 24 folles.

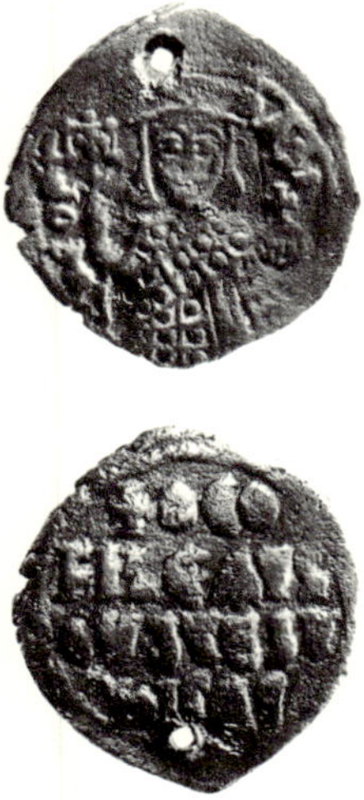

Theophilus

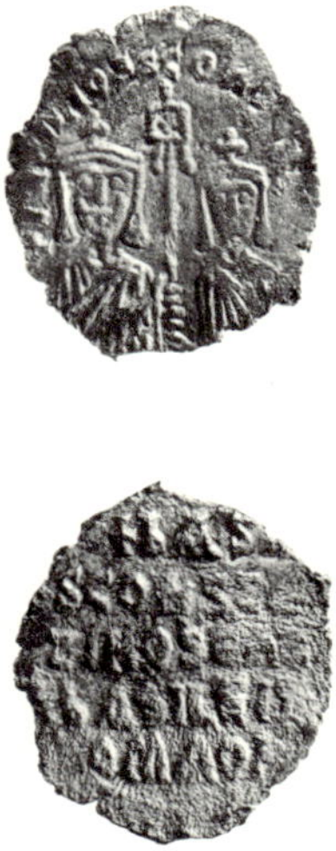

Basil I and Constantine

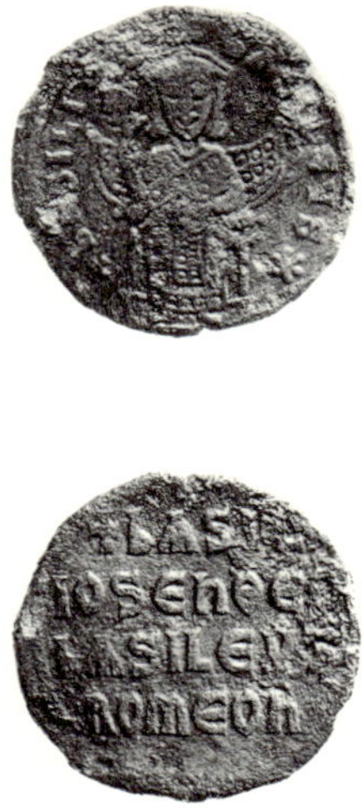

Basil I

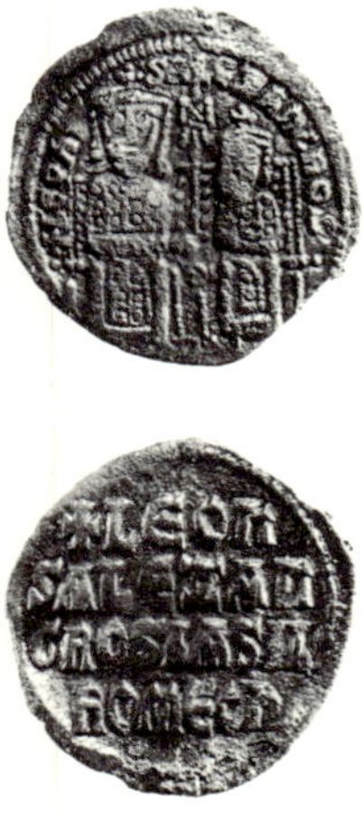

Leo VI and Alexander

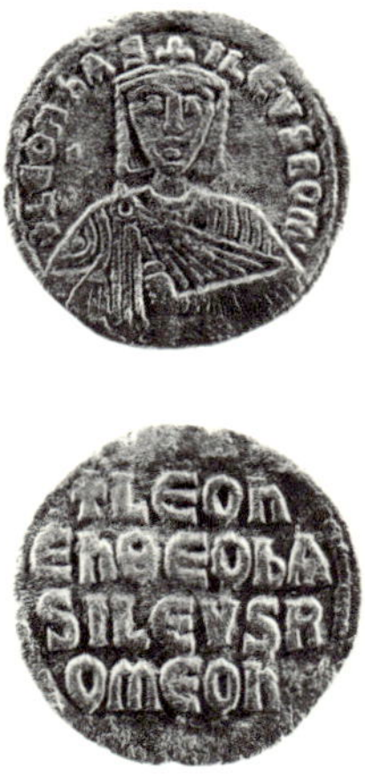

Leo VI

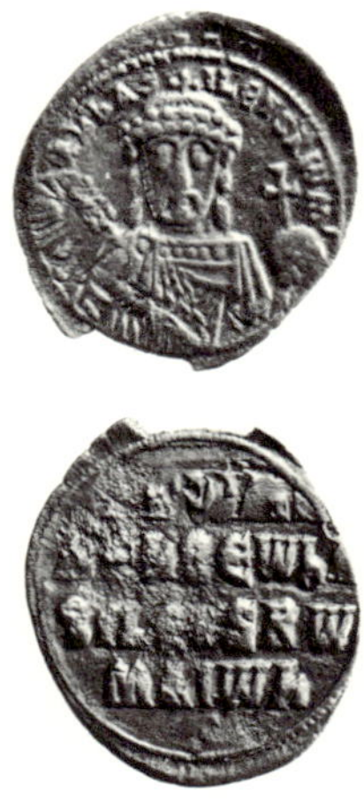

Romanus I

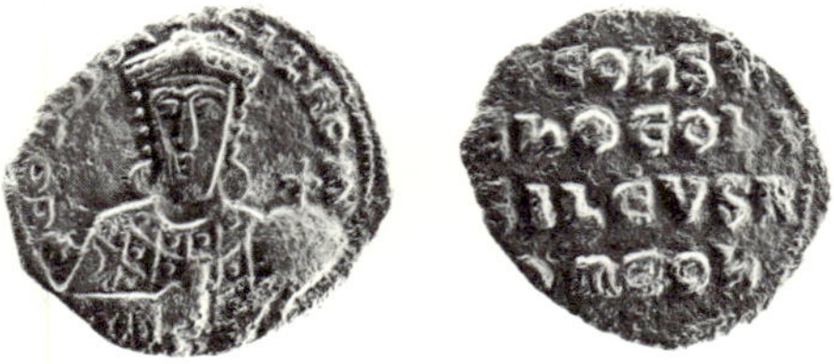

Constantine VII

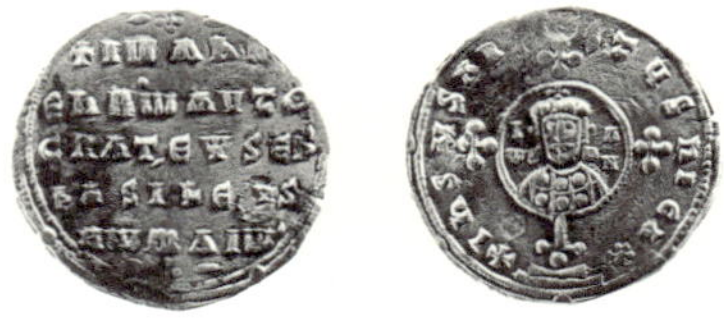

John I

10. 9th- and 10th-century Byzantine coins.

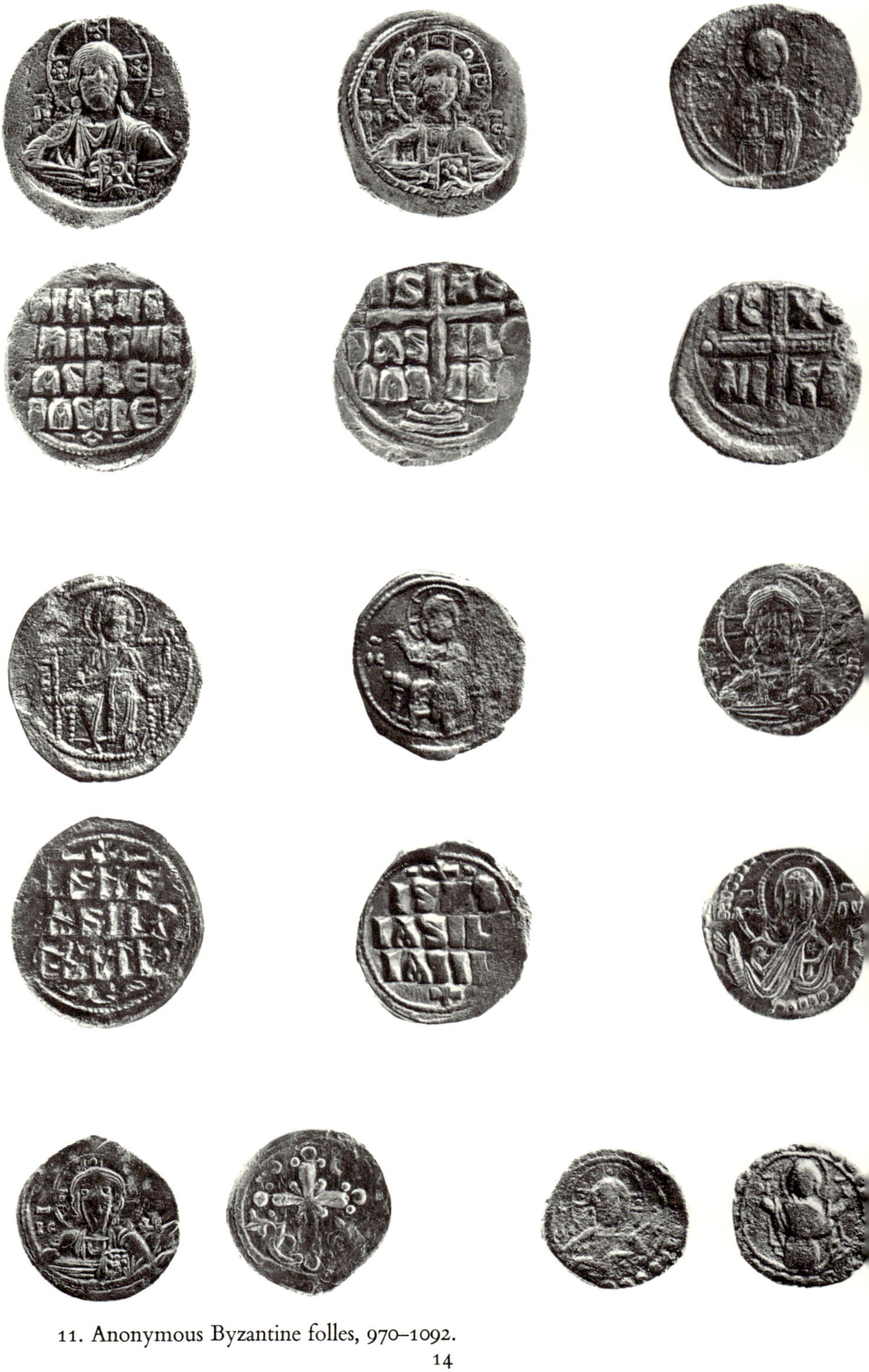

11. Anonymous Byzantine folles, 970–1092.

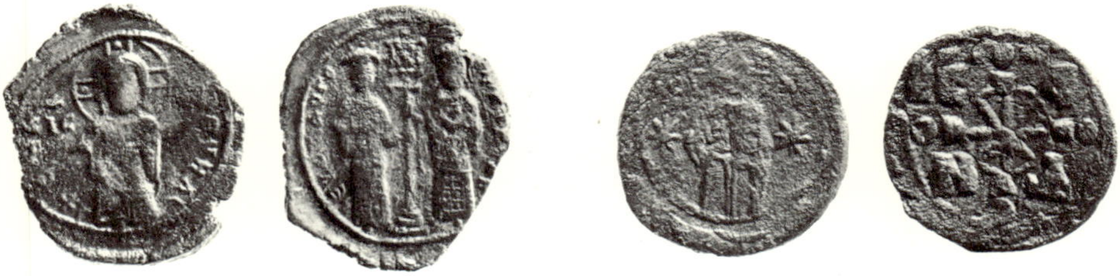

12. Folles of Constantine X and Eudoxia and of Nicephorus III.

During the reign of John I a revolution took place in the design of Byzantine copper coins. A new type, the so-called 'anonymous' follis (11), was introduced and, with modifications, lasted about a century. The new follis derives its name from the fact that the name, titles, and portrait of the emperor were replaced by an image of Christ (and, in some instances, also the Virgin) and an inscription that makes no mention of the current ruler. The exact chronology of the 'anonymous' folles has been difficult to establish because of the absence of imperial names, but scholars are now in agreement as to the sequence of issues and their approximate date. Overstruck specimens excavated in the Agora have been of great value in ordering and dating the several series.

The earliest 'anonymous' folles are similar in general appearance to the folles of the preceding century and carry a frontal bust of Christ on the obverse and a four-line inscription ('Jesus Christ, King of Kings') on the reverse. On later issues Christ appears as a half-length figure or enthroned and the reverse inscription is variously abbreviated. Around 1065–1070 the reverse inscription is replaced by a bust of the Virgin and the legend 'Mother of God' in abbreviated form. An elaborate Latin cross or the seated Virgin appears on the reverses of the latest series.

After *ca.* 1060 the 'anonymous' folles were supplemented by issues that once again bore imperial likenesses and names (or initials), although Christ still figured prominently on the obverses (12). The resumption of 'imperial' issues may have been due to the influence of Eudocia, wife of Constantine X (1059–1067), who appears beside her husband on follis reverses as well as on some issues in precious metal. The 'imperial' folles of Nicephorus III have been found in great numbers in the Agora and bear a representation of Christ and a cross with four letters in the angles that stand for 'may the Cross protect Nicephorus the emperor'.

THE BYZANTINE FOLLIS was abolished by the monetary reform of 1092 instituted under Alexius I Comnenus (1081–1118). After that date the standard small-change coins of the Byzantine Empire were the tetarteron and the half-tetarteron (13). The tetarteron was a small copper coin of thick fabric, lighter even than the reduced-weight folles of the late 11th century. Thousands of tetartera and half-tetartera have been unearthed in the Agora. Most of the excavation pieces date to the reign of Manuel I (1143–1180), when three mints were in operation—one at Constantinople, another at Thessalonica, and a third at an as yet unidentified Greek site, possibly Athens itself.

The types of the new coins are generally similar to those of the pre-reform folles. One of the illustrated tetartera of Alexius bears busts of Christ and the emperor, the other a jeweled cross with initials and a bust of Alexius. The tetarteron of Alexius' son, John II (1118–1143), pairs a bust of Christ with one of the emperor. The two half-tetartera of Manuel are stamped with the emperor's monogram and his portrait, and a cross on steps and imperial portrait, while that of Andronicus I (1183–1185), last of the Comnenus dynasty, carries bust-length images of the Virgin and the emperor. Coins such as these formed the basic currency for small commercial transactions in Athens from the time of their introduction until the middle of the 13th century.

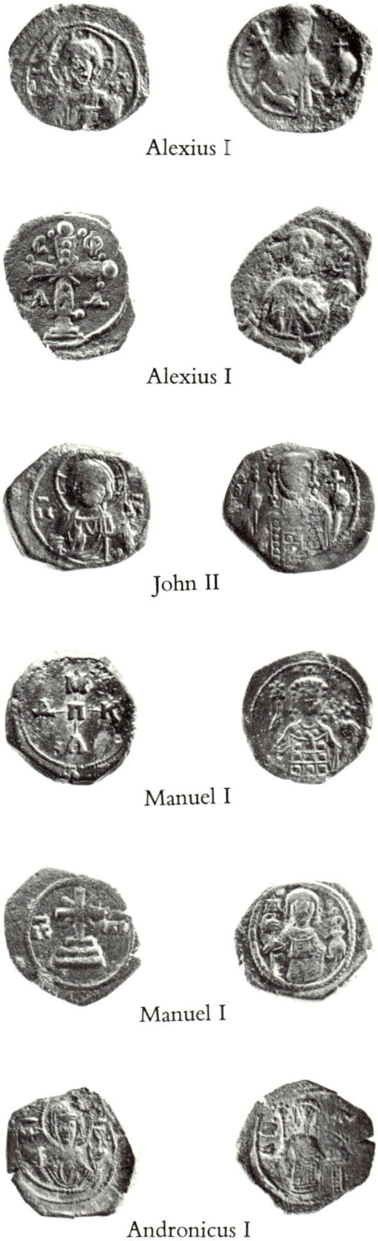

13. Tetartera and half-tetartera of the Comneni, 1092–1185.

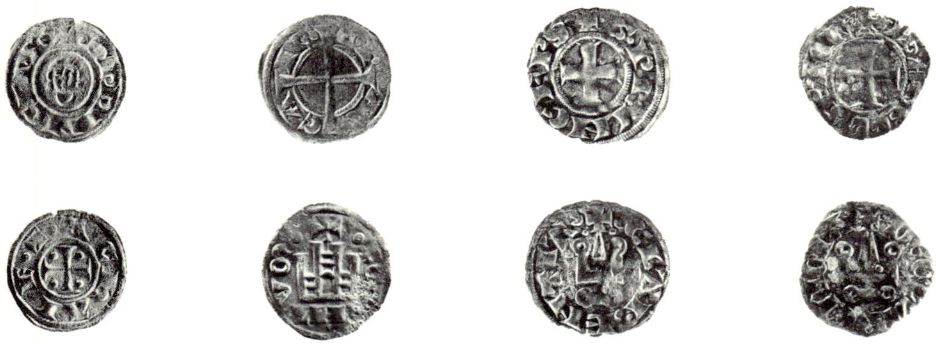

Guillaume II de Villehardouin — Isabelle

14. Coins of the Frankish Principality of Achaia.

COINAGE OF THE LATIN CONQUERORS

After the fall of Constantinople on 13 April 1204 at the hands of the Fourth Crusaders, the great city was sacked and the Byzantine Empire was partitioned by its Latin conquerors. The new Latin Empire established at Constantinople lasted only 57 years, but some of the Latin domains set up in Greece lasted for over two centuries. The Peloponnesos (the Morea) and Attica-Boiotia were allotted to the Frankish crusaders, whose realms came to be called the Principality of Achaia and the Duchy of Athens and Thebes respectively. Under Latin rule Athens became the home of mediaeval knights who held tournaments before the Church of St. Mary of Athens on the Akropolis (the Parthenon).

The first of the Frankish lords of Athens was Othon de la Roche (1204–1225), a Burgundian nobleman. Under Othon and for about the first two

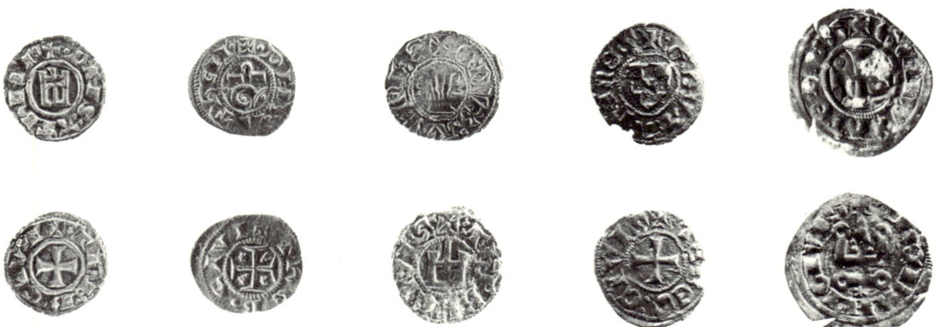

Guy I de la Roche — Guillaume I de la Roche — Guy II

15. Coins of the Frankish Duchy of Athens and Thebes.

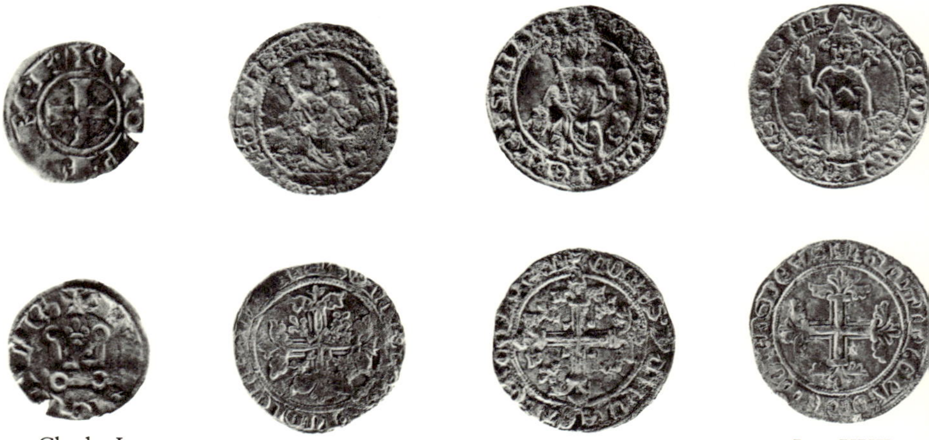

Charles I Charles II Robert Jean XXII

16. 13th- and 14th-century French coins.

decades of the rule of his nephew and successor, Guy I de la Roche (1225–1263), the petty currency used in Athens continued to be the 12th-century Byzantine coppers of the Comneni. Towards the middle of the 13th century, however, Guillaume II de Villehardouin, Prince of Achaia (1245–1278), and Guy I of Athens began to issue their own money. These new Frankish coins have been found in considerable numbers in the Agora excavations (14, 15). They were struck at first only in copper, but around 1267 Prince Guillaume II inaugurated the minting of new higher-denomination pieces in billon (an alloy of silver and copper) and about 13 years later Duke Guillaume I de la Roche (1280–1287) followed suit. Three mints were employed by the Franks for the manufacture of billon and copper coins during this period—Corinth and Clarentzia in the Peloponnesos and Thebes in Boiotia.

The Frankish copper pieces vary considerably in type. A facing head of the prince and a cross with the inscription ACHAIE, and a cross and stylized representation of the castle of Acrocorinth are types used by Guillaume II de Villehardouin (14). Guy I and Guillaume I de la Roche also adopted the cross as a type, but employed in addition a schematic 'Genoese gate' modeled on Italian coin designs, a fleur-de-lis, and a coat-of-arms (15).

The billon types are similar at both the Clarentzia and Thebes mints: a cross and 'castle of Tours'. Illustrated are pieces struck by Guillaume II and Isabelle de Villehardouin (14) and Guy II de la Roche (15). Such Frankish 'deniers tournois' (the name denier is derived from the Latin denarius) are copies of contemporary French coins. Some French deniers tournois have also been found in the Agora, among them a denier of Charles I d'Anjou, Count of Provence (1246–1285) and also Prince of Achaia (1278–1285) (16).

Other contemporary French silver coins occasionally appear in the excavations (16). They are called carlins, after Charles II, Count of Provence (1285–1309), and bear his effigy or that of Robert, Count of Provence (1309–1343) or Jean XXII, Pope at Avignon (1316–1334).

The Latin crusaders who captured Constantinople in 1204 had been transported to the East by a Venetian fleet. The Italian port city consequently received a large share of the territory conquered by the Fourth Crusaders and established maritime colonies throughout the Greek world. A proposal to transfer the seat of government from Venice to Constantinople was even seriously debated, although rejected, by the Venetian Assembly in 1222.

The earliest Venetian coins found in the American excavations (17) are those of Doge Jacopo Tiepolo (1229–1249). One of his silver grossi, with the doge and St. Mark on the obverse and Christ enthroned on the reverse, is illustrated. Nevertheless, during the first 70 years of Latin rule in Greece, Venetian coins are rare in Athens, the monetary needs of the city having been met by old Byzantine coppers and new Frankish currency. A few dozen coins of Francesco Dandolo (1329–1339) and Marco Corner (1365–1367) have, however, been unearthed in the Agora, including the silver soldino of Dandolo and billon tornesello of Corner reproduced here. The civic emblem of

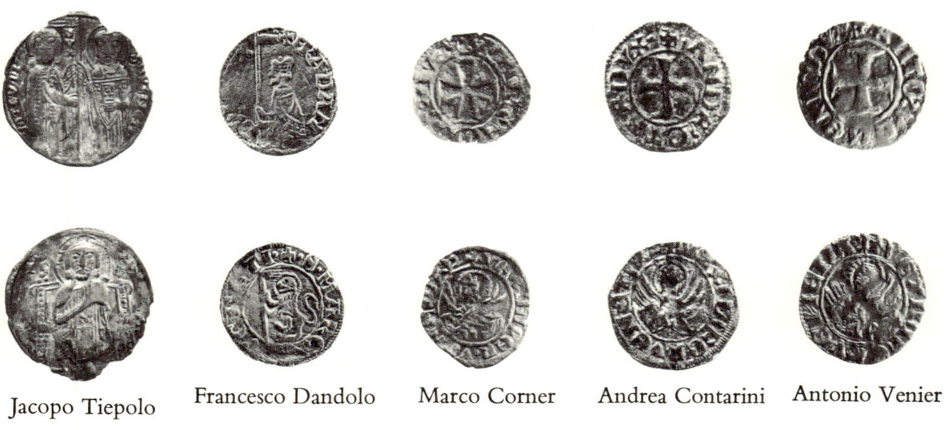

17. Venetian coins, 1229–1400.

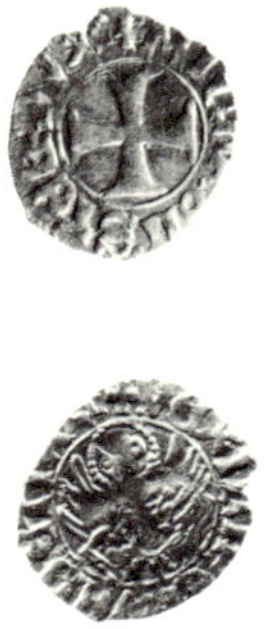

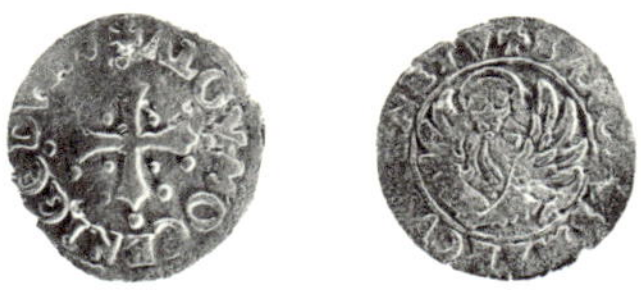

Alvise Mocenigo

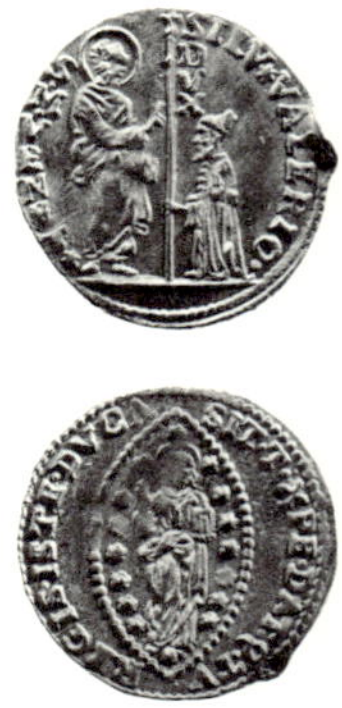

Michele Steno

Silvestro Valier

18. Venetian coins, 1400–1700.

Venice, the lion of St. Mark, figures prominently on these and most other Venetian issues.

After the death of Duke Nerio Acciajuoli in 1394, Athens came under Venetian control and remained a Venetian colony until the city was recovered by Nerio's son Antonio early in 1403. During this period Athens was governed by a Venetian podestà and the chief currency of the city was Venetian. Great quantities of billon torneselli of Andrea Contarini (1368–1382) and Antonio Venier (1382–1400) were brought to Athens and over 300 have been discovered in the Agora (17).

The number of Venetian coins in the Agora falls off sharply beginning with the dogeship of Michele Steno (1400–1413). The excavations have, nevertheless, brought to light about 100 Venetian issues of the doges of the 15th, 16th, and 17th centuries (18). These include a billon tornesello of Steno with the standard cross/lion of St. Mark types, a billon sesino of Alvise Mocenigo (1570–1577), and a ducat (or zecchino) of Silvestro Valier (1694–1700), the only Venetian gold coin found in the Agora. The Venetian sesino has types similar, but not identical, to those of the tornesello. The ducat, struck in 24-carat gold, carries representations of the doge kneeling before St. Mark and of Christ in a mandorla. The reverse inscription reads 'Let this duchy which Thou rulest be dedicated to Thee, O Christ.' Ducats were first struck in Venice in 1284 and their types remained essentially unchanged through the centuries.

In addition to these issues of the doges intended primarily for use in Italy, the Agora finds include Venetian coins minted specifically for use in its colonies (19). Among these are a billon carzia of Lorenzo Priuli (1556–1559)

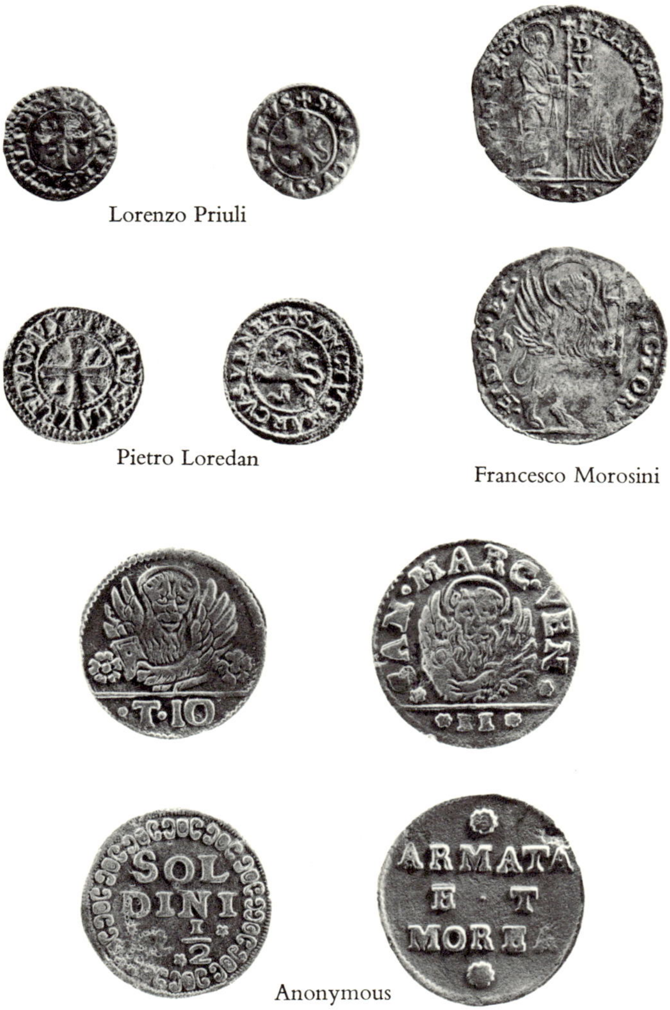

19. 16th- and 17th-century Venetian colonial issues.

and a billon 4-carzi piece of Pietro Loredan (1567–1570) struck for Cyprus during the time that island was under Venetian control (1489–1570). Also illustrated is a silver $\frac{1}{8}$-lion piece, for use in the Levant, of Francesco Morosini (1688–1694), infamous for causing an explosion in the Parthenon when he bombarded the Akropolis. A few hundred anonymous colonial copper issues have also turned up in the Agora, including a 10-torneso ($2\frac{1}{2}$-soldino) piece struck for use in Crete and a gazzetta intended for the Venetian fleet and the Morea.

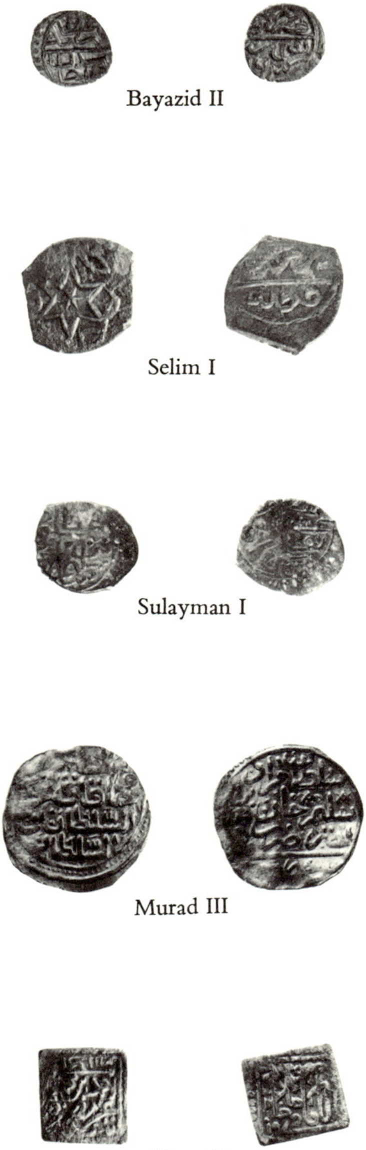

20. Ottoman Turkish coins, 1481–1617.

TURKISH COINAGE

ON 29 MAY 1453 Constantinople fell to the Ottoman Turks under Muhammad II 'the Conqueror' (1451–1481) after a 54-day siege. The city was renamed Istanbul, the name it bears to this day, and a number of great buildings were erected, among them the famous Topkapi Palace and the Grand Bazaar. The conquest of the former capital of the Byzantine Empire was followed quickly by the subjection of all of Greece to the Ottoman Turks. Athens became a part of the Ottoman Empire in January 1459 and before long the Parthenon was converted into a mosque. For almost the next four centuries Turkish coins constituted the basic currency of the Greek city.

Over 6,000 Ottoman coins have been discovered during the course of the American excavations in the Agora (20–22). They are of special interest because they are the only non-Western coins ever to have been used extensively in Greece. The Muslim coins differ from the coins used in Athens before and after the Turkish presence in that, because of religious tenets, they never bear images of persons or objects, but are almost exclusively epigraphic in type. Only occasionally are decorative patterns used and the coin designs are confined essentially to Arabic legends. The coins are consequently unintelligible to those who have not had specialized linguistic training, but they may be appreciated nevertheless for the calligraphic beauty of the finest pieces.

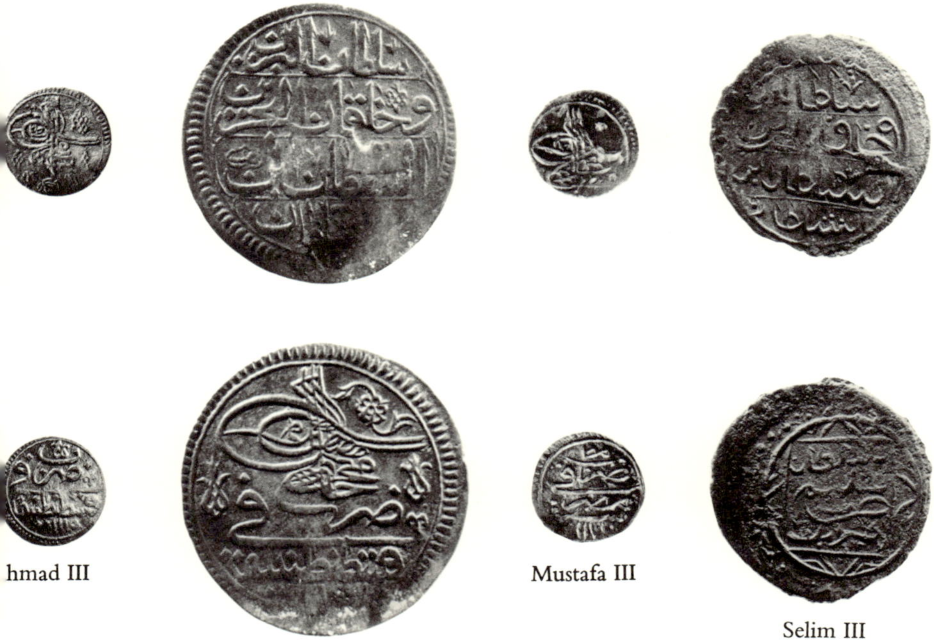

21. 18th-century Ottoman Turkish coins.

The Ottoman issues illustrated here include some rather crude early hammered bronze pieces of irregular shape and others produced by modern minting machinery, as well as several denominations of gold, silver, and copper coins. All the pieces share, however, a number of common features. The name of the current sultan is prominently spelled out in Arabic script, which is read from right to left. The coin type is frequently dominated by the *tughra*, the elaborate official signature of the ruler, as on all but one of the illustrated 18th- and 19th-century pieces (21, 22). The *tughra* contains the sultan's name, the title 'khan' (lord), the sultan's father's name, and the epithet 'al Muzaffer da᾿ma' (the ever victorious). The Ottoman coins, like their Byzantine predecessors in the Agora, are quite informative. They regularly bear the place of minting and, from the time of Mustafa III (1757–1774), the date of issue. The year of striking is determined by the combination of accession year and regnal year stamped on the coins. The dates are given according to the Muslim Era reckoned from the Flight (Hijra) of the prophet Muhammad from Mecca to Medina in A.D. 622. (Muslim years are lunar years. To convert Hijra dates to common-era dates, 97% of the Hijra date is added to 622.) The

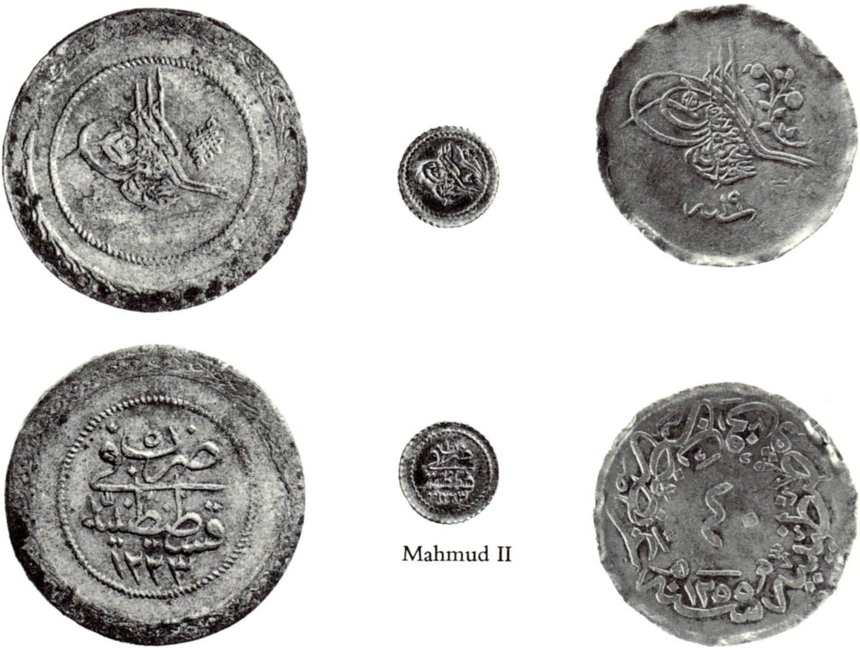

Mahmud II

Mahmud II

ʿAbd al-Majid

22. 19th-century Ottoman Turkish coins.

Turkish pieces also often carry formulaic phrases, such as 'sultan of the two continents [Europe and Asia] and lord of the two seas [Aegean and Euxine]', and 'may his victory be glorious'.

The number of Ottoman coins found in the Agora declines sharply after the Greek War of Independence, but later pieces like that of ʿAbd al-Majid (1839–1861) have been found (22). The two illustrated coins of Mahmud II (1808–1839) come from a hoard found in 1971 containing both Ottoman gold and silver pieces and large silver coins struck in Europe and the Americas. The hoard and stray finds attest that during the period of Turkish domination Western coins also circulated in Athens. In 1933 both Arabic script and Hijra dates were abandoned and Western-style pictorial types were adopted for the Turkish coinage.

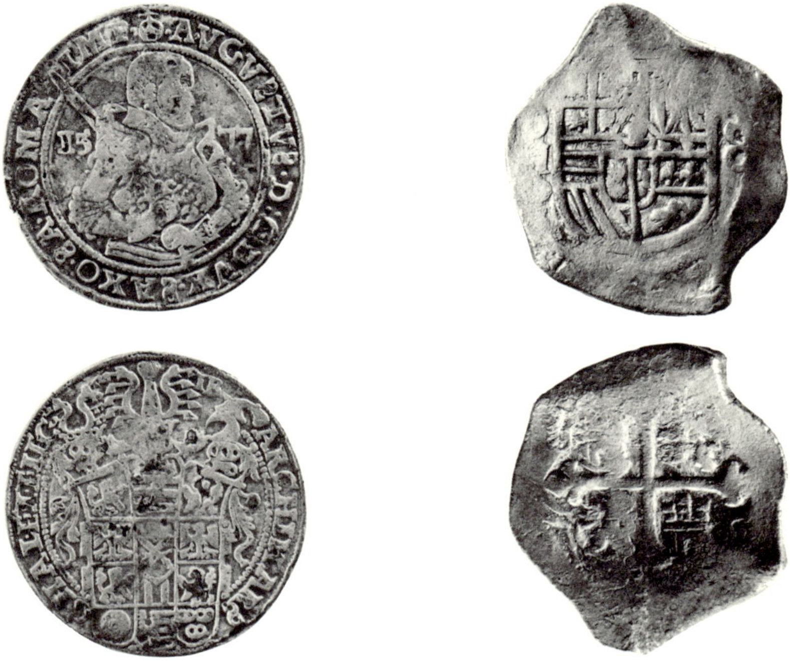

23. A Dresden taler and a Mexico City 8-real piece.

COINS OF WESTERN EUROPE AND THE AMERICAS

ALTHOUGH OTTOMAN MONEY was used for daily commercial transactions in Turkish Athens, coins struck in Western Europe and as far away as Central and South America also found their way into the Athenian market place. Such coins (other than those of Venice) are not frequently encountered in the excavations, but some of those brought to light in the Agora are reproduced here (23–25).

One of the major coins of Western Europe was the silver taler (the root of the English word 'dollar') and from time to time talers have been found in Athens, undoubtedly brought to the Greek city by foreign merchants. Illustrated here is a taler struck in Dresden in 1577 under August, Elector of Saxony of the Albertine line (23). The obverse carries a bust-length portrait of August, who is shown wearing a cuirass and holding a sword; the reverse is stamped with the Elector's coat-of-arms.

The American excavations in the Agora have surprisingly also uncovered a few Spanish silver 8-real pieces minted in Mexico and Bolivia, among them a characteristically poorly struck specimen of Philip IV (1624–1665) with heraldic types, from Mexico City (23). The irregularly shaped 8-real pieces from the New World were struck on flans obtained by slicing silver bars and must have been regarded with suspicion by the few Athenians who encountered them.

The coinage of modern France is well represented by a silver piece struck in 1661 under King Louis XIV, a 20-franc piece (one of a handful of gold coins found in the Agora), minted for Napoleon III in 1854 (24), and a handsome series of silver 5-franc pieces, part of a hoard discovered during the demolition of a modern house in 1937 (25). The French coins from the hoard were found together with a silver piece of Ferdinand VII of Spain and some 19th-century Greek coins. The French pieces date to a time of political upheaval in France and portray successive rulers: the emperor Napoleon Bonaparte, the Bourbon kings Louis XVIII and Charles X, and King Louis Philippe of Orleans. The gold piece of Napoleon III dates to the restored Second Empire. All the coins bear the head, name, and title of the current ruler on the obverse, and the denomination, date, and mint mark on the reverse. The designs of the coins were determined by artistic competitions and the prize-winning artists were permitted to place their signatures on the obverse dies.

24. Coins of Louis XIV and Napoleon III of France.

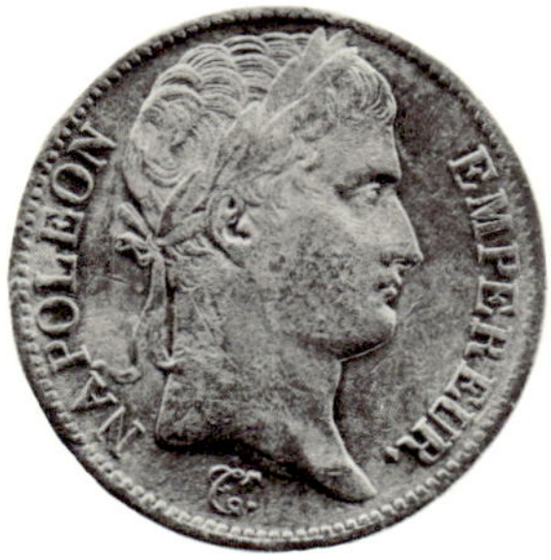

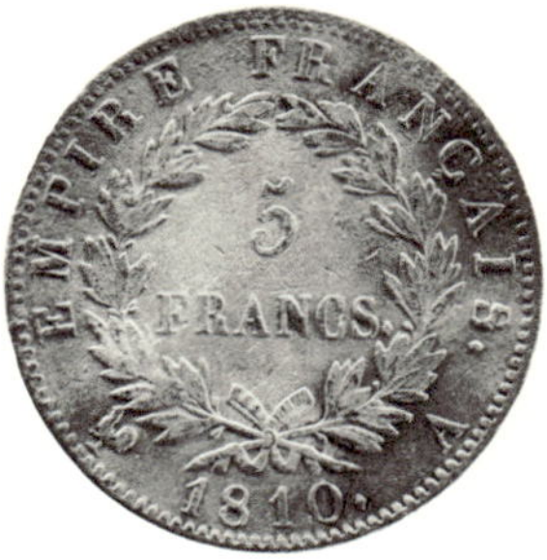

Napoleon

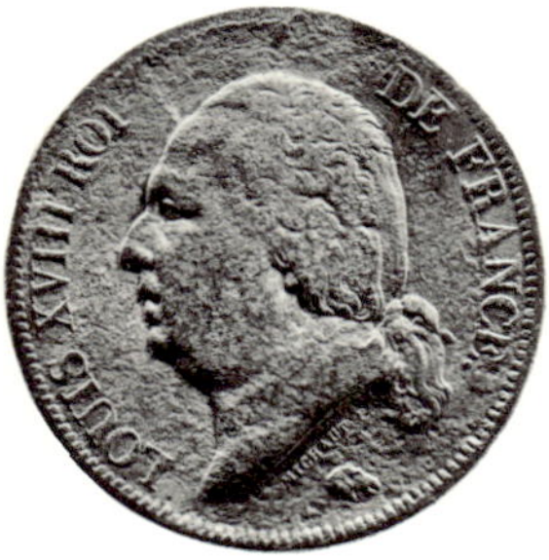

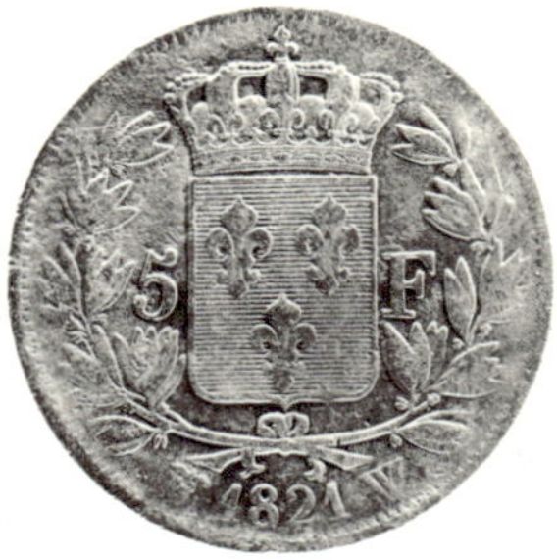

Louis XVIII

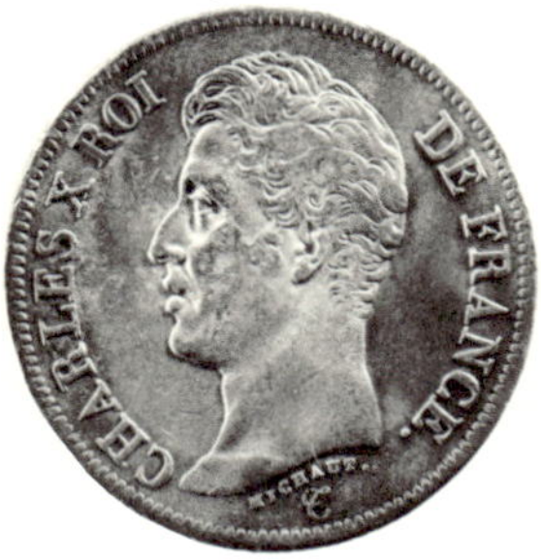

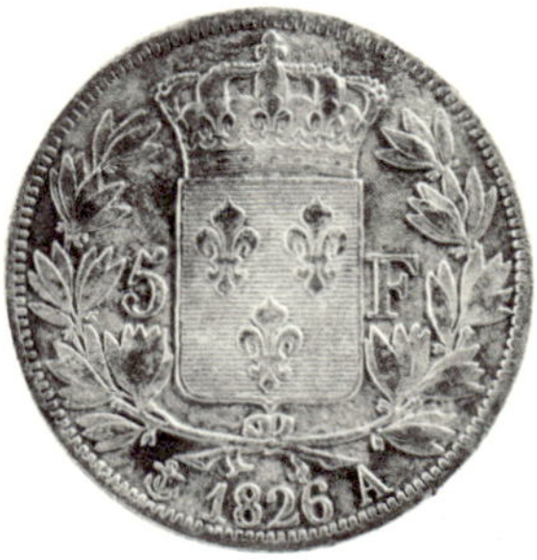

Charles X

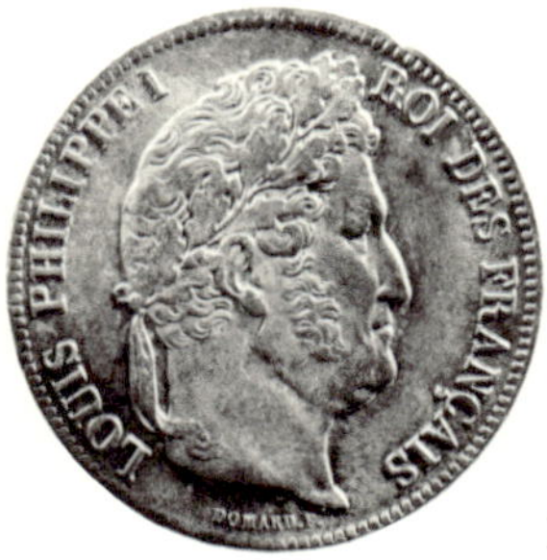

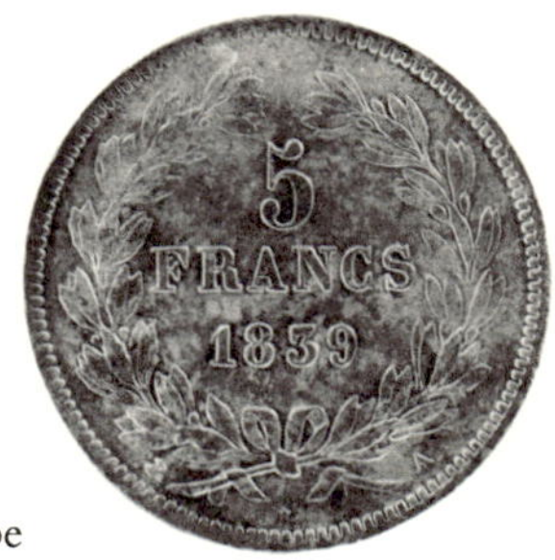

Louis Philippe

25. French 5-franc pieces from a hoard of European and Greek coins.

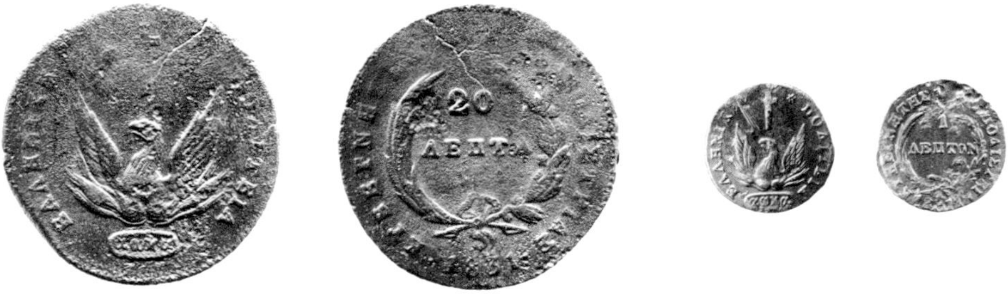

26. Greek coins of John Capodistrias, 1831.

MODERN GREEK COINAGE

On 25 March 1821 the Greeks rose up against their Turkish overlords and began the War of Independence that was successfully concluded in 1827. The next year the first coins of the new Greek nation were issued under President John Capodistrias (26). The unit chosen for the new coins was the phoenix, divided into 100 lepta. Silver 1-phoenix coins and copper pieces ranging in value from one to twenty lepta were struck. The types of both silver and copper coins were, on the obverse, the phoenix above *αωκα* (1821 in Greek numerals) and, on the reverse, the value in a wreath. The phoenix was a fitting symbol for the resurrected Greece—a mythological creature reborn from its own ashes. The coins of Capodistrias were struck on the island of Aigina using an archaic mint press obtained from the Order of St. John on Malta. The silver needed to produce the new coins was supplied by Russia; it is said that the copper was obtained by melting Venetian guns.

After the assassination of Capodistrias in 1831, the great powers of Europe chose the 17-year-old Otho, Prince of Bavaria, as first King of Greece (1832–

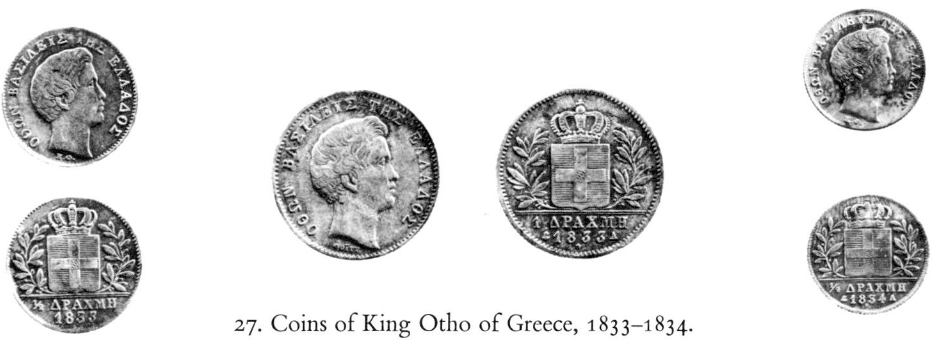

27. Coins of King Otho of Greece, 1833–1834.

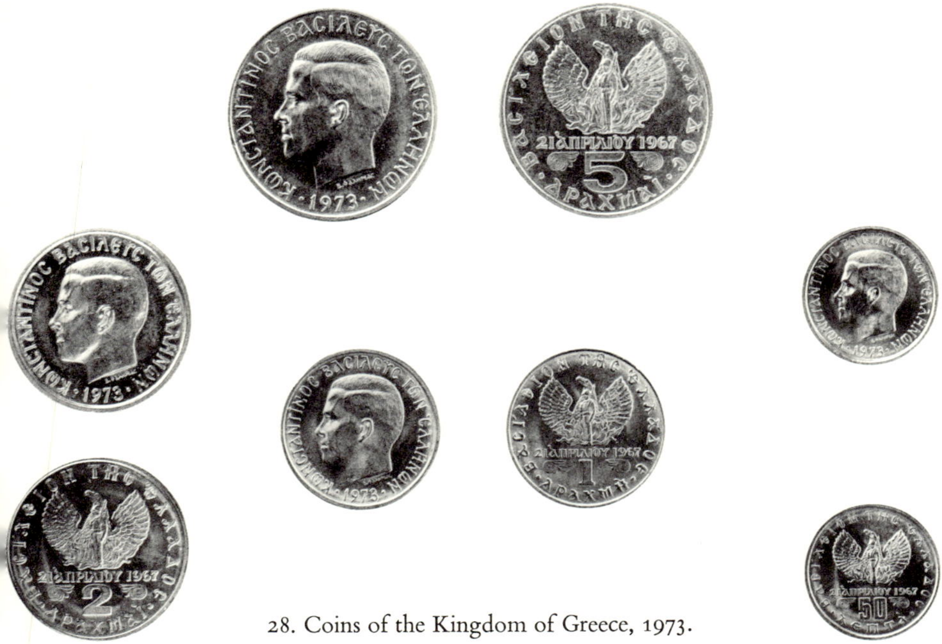

28. Coins of the Kingdom of Greece, 1973.

1862). The new monetary unit of the Kingdom of Greece was the drachma, a revival of the silver unit used in ancient times. The drachma was also divided into 100 lepta. Nine denominations were struck under Otho, ranging from a copper 1-lepton piece to a gold 20-drachma piece. Unlike the coinage of Capodistrias, the new royal coinage was produced in Munich, the capital of Bavaria, and in Paris. The three silver coins of Otho illustrated here (27) come from a hoard of 120 Greek coins found in 1952 in a green cloth bag between the stones of a modern wall. All bear the head of the youthful king on the obverse and the crowned royal arms on the reverse. The reverse dies also carry the denomination, the date, and the mint mark. In 1836 a new mint was established in Athens, but it was closed in 1858. From then until 1971, Greek coins were again struck abroad. The later Greek pieces turn up regularly in the excavations.

The Athenian Agora is today not a market place, but an archaeological site with a museum. Nevertheless, coins still exchange hands in the Agora through the collection of admission fees and the sale of books and souvenirs in the Stoa of Attalos, and coins are undoubtedly still being lost on the site. The coins used in the Agora today (28–30) are, like those of all other centuries of the city's life, important historical documents. The past several years have

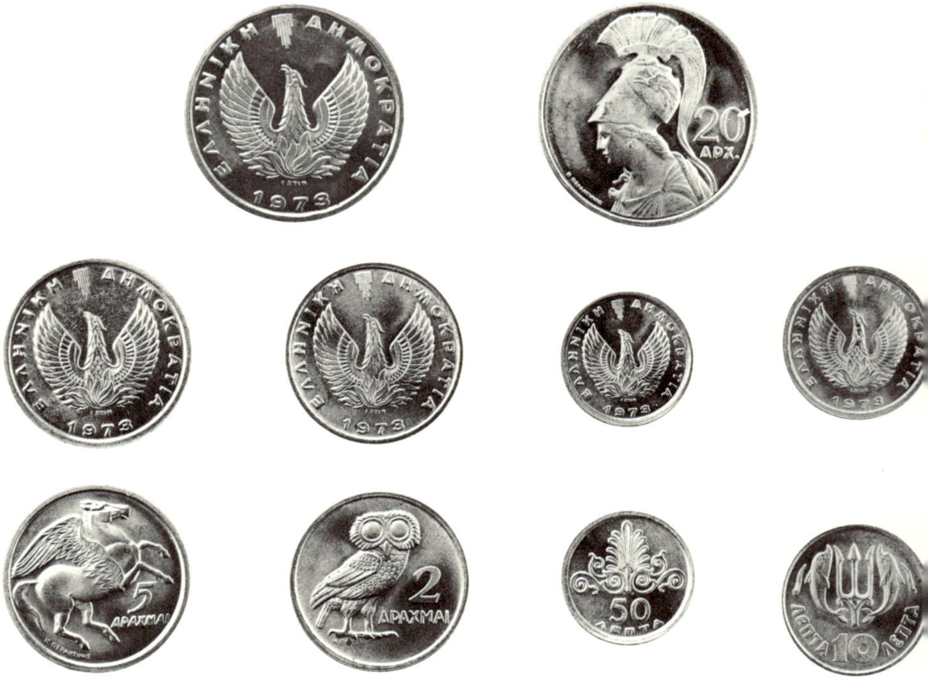

29. Coins of the Greek Republic, 1973.

seen major changes in the country's government and these changes are recorded on the coinage.

On 21 April 1967 the government of King Constantine was overthrown by the military. For a few years the King's coin types—head of Constantine and royal arms—were unchanged, but in 1971 the royal arms were replaced by a new design. The new reverse type, used on all denominations until 1973, recalls that of Capodistrias—a phoenix, accompanied by a soldier, above the date of the revolution (28). Despite Constantine's exile from Greece, the coins continued to bear his portrait on the obverse and the inscription 'Kingdom of Greece' on the reverse.

On 29 July 1973 the Kingdom of Greece officially became the Republic of Greece and new coins were quickly introduced by the military junta (29). The phoenix replaced Constantine's head as unvarying obverse type and the date of the revolution and its symbol (the soldier) were removed, thereby implying the legitimacy of the new government. The reverse types allude to the ancient past of Greece—a detail of a statue of Athena, Pegasos (an ancient

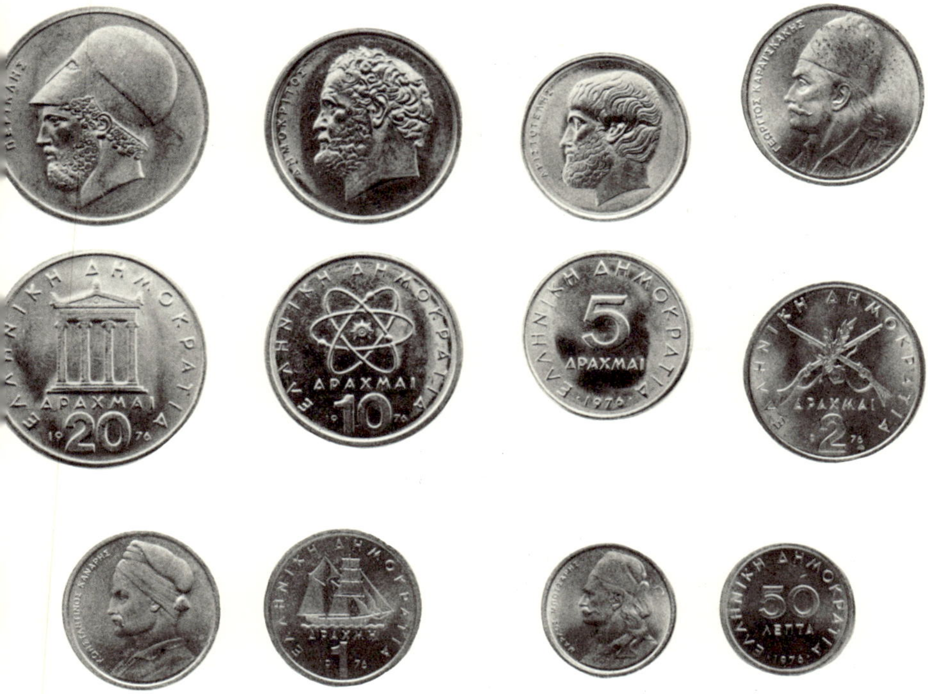

30. Coins of the Greek Republic, 1976.

Corinthian coin type), Athena's owl (used on ancient Athenian coins), ancient architectural ornament, and dolphins framing Poseidon's trident.

The military dictatorship of Greece came to an end on 25 November 1973, but it was not until 1976 that the duly elected officials of the Republic authorized the minting of coins with new types (30). The higher denominations (20-, 10-, and 5-drachma) bear the heads of famous ancient Greeks—Perikles, Demokritos, and Aristotle. The 2-drachma, 1-drachma, and 50-lepton pieces are stamped with likenesses of heroes of the War of Independence—Karaïskakis, Kanaris, and Botsaris.

In years to come other coins will undoubtedly be used in the Athenian Agora and they too will tell the historian much about the life of the city.

ILLUSTRATIONS

All coins illustrated come from the Agora excavations, with the exception of the contemporary Greek coins in Figures 28–30. The inventory numbers of the excavated pieces are given below.

1. Drawing 2283, by Helen Besi.
2. T-766.
3. Σ-3663.
4. B-381, Σ-1712, Σ-4702, A-140, Σ-4328, Σ-793, AA-187, Σ-452, Σ-4466.
5. Σ-648, BB-623, NN-1281.
6. N-476, MM-52, Λ-281.
7. BΓ-467–BΓ-807.
8. BΓ-469, ΛΛ-385, B-306.
9. NSB-199, ΠΘ-513, ΛΛ-248, P-14, ΠΘ-352, Σ-4192, E-2423.
10. Λ-64, Σ-5181, NN-44, ΛΛ-461, Σ-4830, X-203, Σ-4934, P-230.
11. Δ-58, I-321, N-1017, BΓ-8, Γ-186, Σ-5565, AA-696, Π-423.
12. Z-1484, H-2068.
13. Σ-3856, X-23, ΛΛ-477, H-1788, B-28, T-569.
14. Γ-1141, ΠΘ-639, KK-473, AA-591.
15. Fr. hoard 53, H′-3545, Σ-6015, NSB-394, I-1528.
16. NSB-642, I-1488, I-1489, I-1490.
17. I-68, ΠΘ-108, NSB-451, NSC-298, NSB-589.
18. NSB-504, NN-344, N-452.
19. NSB-549, AA-497, H-362, X-11, X-130.
20. GCM-1658.15, GCM-2385.21, GCM-2518.2, GCM-1862bis, GCM-314.37.
21. GCM-985.23, GCM-651.1, GCM-2190.14, GCM-862.28.
22. BΓ-824, BΓ-813, GCM-2519.7.
23. Σ-6504, PP-25.
24. NN-160, E-786.
25. Σ-3557, Σ-3556, Σ-3553a, Σ-3554.
26. NSR-275, NSB-635.
27. T-1814, T-1813, T-1816.